WINDOWS KISS THE SHADOWS OF THE PASSING THIRTY MILLION

by

Robert Golden

ISBN: 978-1-909470-89-7

Published by Triarchy Press
www.triarchypress.net

© Robert Golden 2015

This book is licensed under a Creative Commons Attribution-NonCommercial-NoDerivs 3.0 Unported Licence. Permissions are available from the publishers. You are free to copy, distribute and transmit the work on the following conditions:

You must attribute the work in the manner specified below (but not in any way that suggests the author endorses you or your use of the work).

You may not use this work for commercial purposes.

You may not alter, transform or build upon this work.

Attribution: Golden, Robert, *Windows Kiss the Shadows of the Passing Thirty Million*, Axminster: Triarchy Press (2015)

The right of Robert Golden to be identified as the author of this work has been asserted by him in accordance with the Copyright, Design and Patents Act 1988.

INTRODUCTION

EXILE

Why now – and is it only now – that we face this tragic stream of people being forcibly exiled from their homes, land and countries? Is it because of a band of fundamentalists in Syria and Iraq that this is happening?

No.

It is a manifestation of two even more disgraceful human activities.

Since the early 1980s, when Thatcher and Regan adopted the ultra-right foreign policy of the neoconservatives (which included the idea of a clash of civilisations) and the neoliberal economic policy of globalisation and the privatisation of everything, the consequences have torn their way through the political, social, cultural and economic lives of Americans, Britons, Europeans and much of the rest of the world.

The bloating of the permanent arms economy, the off-shoring of industry to areas of low-waged, oppressed workers, the flat-lining of middle and working class incomes, the new and ever increasing costs of education, the continual assault on the welfare state, the creation of industrialised farming and, with it, the destruction of the family farm, the unfair free trade agreements, the refusal to admit to and help to change global warming and on and on… all these create a litany of short-term policies favouring the wealthy and the American and (to a lesser degree) the British banking establishment and the newly created national security state.

These ideologies – and the policies that emerge from them – have also fostered homelessness, high and continuous unemployment, and a mass of rootless people tramping within and across Europe and the United States as well as the Middle East. Combine those things with the endless wars that rage and the result is a renewed and greater crisis in which the destitute are now joined by the terrorised.

During a public meeting, someone asked me who I would allow across our borders – people fleeing terror or kids who want a better job? I said it was our democratic and humane responsibility to judge the policies of our leaders and the wealthy, not the victims of their oppression.

In his 1970 novel *Mr Sammler's Planet* Saul Bellow spoke of "a conspiracy against the sacredness of life". It begs the question: what overriding idea or concept do we presently have that can bind all of us, this loose league of humanity, together?

I would wish the answer to be universal. We know that Mahatma Ghandi, Martin Luther King and Nelson Mandela presented and represented ideas of equality, freedom and justice for all, which influenced many others beyond their own countries. Perhaps, with the help of the Internet, it may also be possible for us to find identity, common cause and solace across great distances, unregulated by local conditions, governments and media corporations.

But how can a nation, a region, a people, a group or an individual identify with a common cause? Too often in the past we have seen the emergence of simplistic, destructive codes of blood, race, nationalism and other ideologies of hatred. Read history carefully and you discover these 'conspiracies against the sacredness of life' arise from economic inequality, formulated or at least supported by the wealthy and their politicians to divert people from understanding that the true enemies of peace and justice are usually their own bankers, politicians and munitions makers.

Fortunately there have also been positive forces at play, forces motivated by and emerging from the common experience of suffering and desiring a better life which recognises that progressive change is only possible if the improvement is for all. Whatever these movements have been called throughout history they have always about one thing – a shared and honoured existence accepted by those who believe in the values of a person-centred rather than a god-centred world in which the needs of the individual and the group, of the majority and the minority are always treated with equal respect. Whatever it is called, it arises in our common humanity.

Previously religion and various 'isms' played the part of providing positive communal values. In most of these cases, whether within Christianity, Islam, Nazism, Communism or Fascism, there was an inseparable and malignant belief that sanctified their own believers while excluding others. This creation of the OTHER has always provided the fuel to destroy those who are not included in the definition of 'true believer'. This process, which is fundamentalism, has always been an enemy of reason, peace and communal trust.

Fundamentalism appeals to the heart while disregarding the mind. It is a cheap rabble-rousing pitch designed to seduce the thoughtless, ill-informed, disgruntled and frustrated masses with a set of simple solutions, while diverting attention away from the real causes of their unhappiness. Witness politicians appealing to national myths rather than admitting to the failure of their own foreign and domestic policies.

In Europe there has been, until recently, at least a partially held post-Enlightenment, post-World War Two set of political and cultural values concerned with the need for personal freedom, equality under the law, fair play and equal opportunity. But the rise and then the failure of neoliberal economics, spawning, as it has, gross inequality, unfairness and self-interested sociopathic discordance throughout society has damaged the previous, short-lived idealism of unifying humanism.

Meanwhile many social democrats, trade union leaders, intellectuals, artists and academics – those who should know better – have bent their knees to the rich and powerful as if their rule is our fate, allowing the natural working class desire for fairness and change to be circumscribed and diluted through false political promises and the periodic cycle of electoral politics. The left has been silenced by the overwhelming wealth of the rich and made uncertain about its own beliefs. The left has forgotten history and forsaken its leadership role in the general progress of human history.

What then has been offered in place of the sacredness of life? We have been seduced by the hollowness of consumerism and then by an adoration of new technologies.

To move forward we need to remember what Milan Kundera wrote in his novel *The Book of Laughter and*

Forgetting, that "the struggle of man against power is the struggle of memory against forgetting".

Meanwhile we twist our hands and ask, 'what can we do about these poor people?', when Anglo-American foreign wars, economic and trade policies and unregulated economic policies every day create more and more human victims.

This poem comes out of this adversity.

I

VOICE ONE

This land stretches from the Urals to the Atlantic
under the stars and eternal debris
spewed into airless space,
silent space,
where for the lack of gravity
no sounds are heard.

VOICE TWO

Below,
men and women of various ages
shuffle across a dusty plain,
unwelcome by locals,
pitied by few,
accepted by less but offered work by one or two –
those who see a strong arm and a weak bargaining position.

VOICE THREE

As they trammel and splash,
there echoes along the granite valley,
off the river's stones,
through the woody restaurant,
pinging off crystal glasses
– sentinels of other's celebrations –
a low and tinkling moan:

SINGER

Oh Gertie I'm failing.

VOICE ONE

These people wearing raggedy black,
march along the mountain's ridges,
the river's banks,
the heat-soaked antediluvian plains,
witnessed with suspicion from afar
by those who have not had
the rhythmic certitude of their lives
broken by the winds of change,
and they, the suspicious onlookers –
field, shop and hearth bound,
smug in their isolation,
wondering,
Are these wild shaggy beasts
of the mountains, seas, fields or farms?

VOICE THREE

None nor neither!
They rose from stone hewn as building blocks,
bricks piled as chimneys,
from church bell towers and city squares,
from iron ore and steel bessemers,
from car plants and the pilings of bridge pylons,
from land once theirs and full with harvests,
now scarred by other's giant combines;
and the marchers knew full well as they marched,
they were of civilisation not savagery
and to them

cobbles and traffic,
hubbub and cement,
culverts and welding,
jack hammers and tarring
were their natural environs.

VOICE ONE

Only the wildest dreams of contented men,
rested men,
fat men,
dreamers that dream and eat,
dreamers with shoes on their feet,
dreamers who drink to forget,
could embrace the raw wind,
the boiling clouds,
the swarming insects,
the cold fevered damp dryness
as being a romantic notion.

VOICE TWO

The marching people knew –
    unlike the peeping observers –
that they belonged inside the squares of human habitation
and not within the winds and wilds.

SINGER

This land stretches from the emerald runes of Eire
where horses grazed upon rolling hills of home
to the edgy hump-back Eurasian Urals
where iron ore was mined.

II

VOICE TWO

From there to here
these people enter the fringes of towns
where gatekeepers inspect them,
looking for disease,
pilfering their pockets
taking what they please
and send them round to the coquille gate,
an open shell...

VOICE ONE

....in a civilisation of metaphor...

VOICE TWO

....an open shell,
ribbed like the fingers of an opened hand
where a bowl of watery soup –
   water clean or not –
and scraps of cabbage float,
and a bed of dirty straw
provided by the good parishioners
await,
while their disease…

VOICE THREE

….is it unemployment?

VOICE ONE

Aids?

VOICE THREE

or leprosy?...

VOICE TWO

…is tolerated,
but the gatekeeper,
the warden,
the good wife,
the cops,
the council officials,
the rich man –
    and his mayor –
warn with finger raised…

VOICE THREE

….Don't overstep the mark,
don't look at my daughter's face,
don't ask for a job or a hand-out,
for you with no fixed address
are not to be trusted,
so eat your fill,
sleep,
and scatter back to the hills.

VOICE ONE

And off the stable's broken plaster
splatters a sound like falling glass.

SINGER

Oh Hanna I'm failing…

III

VOICE ONE

In this Europe
fire became light-bulbs,
shouts became telephones,
words became moveable type,
shadows became photographs,
photographs became games and the games became cinema,
pain became an opiate,
infection became penicillin,
light became energy
and energy light,
and a bird and a dream became a pilot and a plane.

VOICE TWO

And Dante,
sitting on a mountain,
seeing from above through clouds,
seeing below cultivation and civilisation,
seeing as god could see –
>   pattern,
>   creation,
>   death,
>   relationships between spirit and flesh.

VOICE THREE

And in an invention of himself
he admitted to what he felt,
that he was not a shadow,
a smooth and polished creature
with semi-precious stones for eyes,
a face stamped with god's reflective dyes,
a face without character
drawn to mirror the holy one's perfection
gilded in his glory,
but like god –
    a being complete –
and in one moment of self-consciousness
Dante gave god good grounds to vacate Europe.

VOICE ONE

In the reflection of Dante's death mask –
    marble limpid cool sky reflecting –
Michelangelo and Raphael
drew,
carved
and reinvented themselves,
and while artists paid service and painted
the he of Jesus,
the she of Mary
and made certain
the figure of god –
    or his son,
    or his wife –
were inscribed,

trapped in the painting's boundaries –
    fighting the composition's geometry,
but look,
look at their changing faces
as the centuries wore on,
Caravaggio replaced the nobles with the humble,
huddled before in shadows
now at least glazed by shafts –
    a harmony of light and shadows
    announcing quietly
    a humming from a distant hive –
this begrudging hidden history.

IV

VOICE TWO

A marcher in his previous life:
Sunday best,
girl on arm,
a litre of wine,
a bit of local tuck –
    lamb in almond sauce,
    peppers with salted capers,
    trotters layered with sauerkraut and caraway,
    herrings slathered with cream –
then a little Sunday culture at the Academia
and while he slips his arm around her waist he sees
in oil thick with coloured harmonies
not a god the figurehead,
not the one who vacated Europe,
but a man in pain,
a woman in pain,
a disciple in pain
and the marcher-to-be,
the wanderer to be –
    rare gristle in brassy melting pot -
seeing these things,
recognised his forbearers,
his singular self

in that pain
with those tears
in horror,
in death.

VOICE THREE

Now he with his fellows
leave their modest rest –
    that straw and bowl under the open hand –
these people,
once welders,
platers,
plumbers,
furnace gritters,
heave men on the docks,
sailors,
tar layers,
coal miners,
wheel house mates,
these marchers hobo across Slovenia,
Albania, Scotland and France...

VOICE ONE

....and again and again
 like the humming of heated lead
vibrating off the border guard's shed...

SINGER

Oh Matilde I'm failing…

V

VOICE TWO

The sheep of the lowlands,
the fine tools of Prague,
the lenses of Jena,
the oil of Norway,
the wheat of England and butter of France…

VOICE ONE

….once produced and reproduced by the marchers
and theirs before them,
but taken from them as if they were witness to,
rather than makers of,
and someday yesterday or tomorrow,
in another's life or yours or theirs,
these stolen goods and claims renounced
return in obscure ways
via the schoolmen philosophers
Erasmus, St. Augustine, Averroes, St Just
via those who rediscovered the source –
    Aristotle and his pupil Plato
    and all the rest –
Blake, Byron and Berger
in kernels of civilisation
where the ideas
    if not the practice,

where the promise
    if not the delivery
illuminate the marchers with notions of their humanity,
beyond bickering, bartering and other inanities.

VOICE TWO

Now the mines are closing,
the mills are closing,
their suppliers –
    short-order cook quick frying his bacon,
    the stationery merchant counting his pens,
    the school cleaner proud of his kids,
    the teacher, plumber, chemist and clerk –
rationalised and walking across another hill,
remembering:
'don't look at my daughter,
don't tarry too long',
and locals hear them crying...

SINGER

Oh Maudie I'm failing…

VI

VOICE ONE

Every morning, as the sky lighted towards spring,
the men awoke to the blackbirds,
meadowlarks
sea gulls, donkeys and ducks,
whimpering dogs and lowing cows
and insects always hungry for their sweat or blood,
all of whom broke into the marchers' dreams
    of Maudie or Mary,
    of venting steam or laying beams,
    of lusty moments and hearty beers,
breaking in and leaving them like boats adrift
swamped with tears.

SINGER

Ahh coming to light…

VOICE TWO

….said some
but others claimed…

VOICE THREE

It's the earth crying itself awake
with tears of hunger and pain,
as we do each morning of our journey.

VOICE TWO

A marcher,
    once an x-ray technician,
a man who had day by day
penetrated skin and viewed bones and truth –
    mostly unwanted –
sat on his bottom,
legs flat on the damp weeds,
stretching this way and that,
remembering each morning…

VOICE THREE

….when he rolled away from his pink wife,
    he'd place his feet flat on the sunshine carpet –
        warm and slightly scratchy –
    and exhaled a sound of complaint
    as his day bumped into his life…

VOICE TWO

…and his life into his dread of passing time,
    time he wished to grasp like an x-ray –
        transparent,
        fixed –
and he would for that moment ask…

VOICE ONE

….how close are others to me and they to each other?
What divisions exist between us?

VOICE TWO AND THREE
How do we touch each other?

VOICE TWO
As the file of black-coated marchers
endured another muddy course,
a man who knew buses and books
asked his hungry neighbour:

VOICE THREE
What can we know boyo?

VOICE ONE
Only what we see;
for the rest –
    the intuition of motive,
    the mysterious chemistry of the soul,
most of us know these things
as we know those distant hills –
    a place that hides someone else's house.

VOICE TWO
The busman placed a hand on either temple and pressed,
the hungry neighbour pulled his beard
and remembered the waters of a pregnant river.

VOICE THREE
For the mensch amongst us,
those filled with human culture –
who hold these things as the ground-works of goodness:

hype is theatre against emptiness,
life is chaos connected by incident,
and each of us goes alone to our grave.

VOICE ONE

But within his restive body of fear,
he, the rare mensch,
chooses to believe rather than not,
that what we do,
> this marching,
> searching,
> begging,
> hoping
> and hiding in each forest

will bring us back our bread and plates,
our families,
schools and suitable fates.

VOICE TWO

The busman brooded:

VOICE THREE

I'm simple in assumption,
I always return to a single question:
> do I choose a life absurd with painful contradictions,
> and if so
> does that mean I've chosen hope –
>> this endless marching like meander's army,

or do I choose the nothingness of being,
meaning I'll have chosen death?

VOICE TWO

The older man,
    grey beard limp
    stomach groaning,
smiled,
touched the busman –
    a reader of books –
and said he was tired,
with little more to speak.

VOICE ONE

And in the distance,
rebounding from the valley walls –
    luminous with plummeting waterfalls –
memories sang insistently:

SINGER

  Oh Cassia my love
  I'm failing…

VII

VOICE ONE

Shoulder to shoulder walk emptiness and hope
anxiously searching for a way to cope,
but something more
cloaked in the wilds of dreams –
    our fantasy of perfectibility found in our schemes...

VOICE THREE

….for the good life...

VOICE TWO

….not a mensch's life…

VOICE THREE

….a stroll with the pram,
washing the car,
the pension well planned,
the anorak and lace all cleaned and starched –
    a life of little common dreams,
    a life of simple venial truths.

VOICE ONE

But falling short of poetry.

VOICE THREE

The sweet perfume of our lover's skin,
our children's innocent blood,
secrets shared by mothers with their daughters,
when she –

    our winter white and summer pasture –
was confirmed,
and he,

    learning to shave under father's guiding hand,
leans forward to speak god's guiding words,
and as a man to bid and behave.

VOICE ONE

The marchers' retinas held mythic sights
writ indelibly by the old blue tube –

    blips scanning 50 fields a second –
flickering sports,
weather,
soaps,
gossip and news
where big-jawed men and buxom women
power dressed and fit for hungers
became announcers, personalities, chatterers –

    events in themselves and opinion makers –
all webbed
as if the tangle of news and views
were joined at the forehead in the broadcaster's booth.

VOICE TWO

A marcher,
leaving the inner eye for distant lives and loves,
on a morning when he pulled on his socks
next to a sighing woman,
a summer afternoon when he saw a butterfly
struggle from the mouth of his sleeping child,
a wet winter evening before Christmas
when his manager said:

VOICE THREE

No more work boys,
closing down.

VOICE TWO

Or the blurred days and nights
when he heard the social worker say:

VOICE THREE

Got'ta take the kids away,
wife sick,
    take the kids,
dirty dishes,
    take the kids
no one to cook,
the grandma's a drunk,
broken windows
loss of pride,
    take the bairns away,
no better than scroungers off the state –

   living off the state,
   living off their children's pain –
take their kids away.

VOICE ONE

The marchers remembered
with memory like a passing feather,
they once existed
   in the outer world of the manager, clerk,
   accountant and landlord,
   in the inner world of wives and children,
   friends and neighbours,
and as all of these links and memories fell away
   like the passing of a feather in the rain,
their existence –
   held fast in the memory of others –
fell away,
and day by day,
hill by valley,
memory and lived life became misted
in dreams and distant vistas
and in the furthest recall of televisual images,
and they began to exist only inside their pain
and in their recollection of having been seen by others,
and each guttered like candles against the driving rain –
   limpid waning reflections –
memories visited in an unlit corridor
which echoed the marchers' imprisoned perceptions...

SINGER

Oh Steffania,
I'm failing…

VIII

VOICE ONE

Amongst their ranks,
the old shop stewards and autodidacts
worried their souls with asking:

VOICE THREE

Why across centuries of philosophers,
spiritual leaders,
revolutionaries and dreamers
has no one given us an answer?

VOICE TWO

Why us?
Why must we marchers trudge
in this century
after so much hatred and pain –
    from place to place –
distant from our homes,
food,
families and one time jobs,
to search –
    as if beggars –
when it had been us and our forefathers...

VOICE THREE

…who built the cathedrals,
laid the pylons,
cabled the telegraph,
forged the cannons,
fought and died for empire,
country,
city,
religion,
ideology,
racial superiority,
the right to speak our language…

VOICE ONE

…or impose our language on others.

VOICE TWO

Why,
when all that we have built for tomorrow,
and now –
   in that tomorrow –
our reward is to wander forever?

VOICE ONE

In their stomachs and sinewy loins they dreamt:

SINGER

Let me build a hut,
let me build a house,
let's construct together,
while our Germans lay their bricks,

our English construct their dry walls faster,
and our Italian masons mason and plaster.

VOICE THREE

We know,
we have experienced and practised eyes –
    remember the rocks of the castle were hauled by us –
we were grazed and cut and sometimes crushed –
    remember we were always hungry,
    thirsty, hot and filthy,
remember we had no medicine
    save the wise women's wisdom and wonders.

VOICE ONE

They, those women of charity and hope –
    driven out,
    hunted down by the state –
which produced doctors with authority
    to control our bodies,
and lawyers –
    sons of landlords –
to command our labour.

VOICE THREE

Remember,
later we fashioned missiles and drones,
and now we watch their ascent
but you forget it is we who dug the ore,
formed the models,
tuned the pistons,
gave them flight.

VOICE TWO

Once we lived off the earth,
out of the sea,
from the air
that surrounded us,
we had nothing more than humble skills and aptitudes
which we applied to extract sustenance
from the cage of nature.

VOICE THREE

Within that cage we hunted the game,
clothed and fed ourselves
and slowly as the reign of our habitats
spread down from the hills and across the valleys,
we pushed back
the uncertain nightmares of witch-filled forests,
and slowly we pushed back
the lair of the animals,
but still there were moments
when our ancient relatives fluttered with fear
as day passed away by flowing flocks of migrating birds.

VOICE ONE

And have you heard the shouts of battle on the air?
Guttural liquid rushing,
masking unmanly screams of terror,
screams louder than the cracking of bones,
louder than the baying of hounds?

VOICE TWO

So that our titled masters
could extend their rights of ownership
or pay homage to their kings and priests,
but we did so under threat –
   duty bound,
   terror bound,
like stags downed by hounds…

VOICE ONE

….so could we proclaim...

VOICE TWO AND THREE

….no!

VOICE ONE

Breaking our sacred bond with the church
   which looked after our souls,
breaking our earthly bond with our lord
   who protected my fellows and I?
Were we to refuse to pay
the tithes of our corn and cabbage and rent?

VOICE THREE

After their first night with our wives!

VOICE TWO

So off to war we went,
and were ever thankful to the church for our return,
and ever thankful to the lord for his protection.

VOICE ONE

Later we filled the air with chimney smoke
rising from our great coal belching machines
and then the effluent of coke and smelted ores
and chemical metals and slake,
until the fog in our cities choked our children
and the manufactures, bankers and merchants,
realising which winds swept the valley clean,
moved to higher ground in the west
leaving our relatives the smog-bound rest.

VOICE THREE

And when Hitler tormented our western skies
with the ash of millions,
a different fog squatted on our land of Europe
in its long unsettled serpent swirls…

VOICE TWO

and along the country lanes and autobahns,
all the road markings, signals and signs were gone,
and with hands adrift like our souls,
we begged to ask the way.

SINGER

How could they?
Imbued with the enlightenment and renaissance
books and rules,
libraries and courts,
science and its proofs,
how could they?

VOICE ONE

Beethoven, play to us in your ode to joy,
Rilke, tell us what you learn
    from whom so ever speaks to you in the night,
Goethe, write to us in your understanding of love,
Mozart, send us a note through your
Jewish collaborator Heine.
Where are you all in this night and fog
that we can no longer use you as proof…

VOICE THREE

…. that we Europeans
are not polluted by what we and ours have done,
    slowly poisoned with disease
    for our bits of white goods
    leicas and vans
    religious and racial purity?

VOICE TWO

And off the beaten marchers' bodies failing,
spatter uttered words in pains appalling

SINGER

Oh Olga my memory's dim
I'm failing…

IX

VOICE ONE

The marchers wear black
because they mourn their passing ignorance,
they know the reward for their souls will be in heaven –
    the church tells them so,
    Moses and Mohammed,
    priests and popes tell them:
the tomorrow of their demise is the tomorrow of their reward.

To die well in god is to be rewarded in the churchman's eyes,
a gamble many take
in their jihad for Jesus or whom so ever,
that tomorrow
    hope, reward and death are one,
while today,
    suffering their living hell and truth
is another wager
between which they must choose.

For all of them
their step by step march was a different here and now,
which,
in the sizzling pain,
the rolling of empty stomachs

and the searing aloneness of their hearts at night,
reaffirmed –
    moment by moment –
that whatever else was unclear
they were alive …

VOICE TWO

…. but off the darkening river's mirror
they heard the moonlit water cry ever clearer...

SINGER

Oh Aida my child's mother
I'm failing…

X

VOICE ONE
One day the marchers found themselves
at the entrance to a tunnel.
Behind them lay the cities
where men and women showed them no pity,
to whom and where they knew they couldn't return…

VOICE TWO
…. and some mumbled:

VOICE THREE
Home.

VOICE ONE
Some murmured:

VOICE THREE
…. It's around the next hill.

VOICE ONE
Others shouted:

VOICE TWO
….It'll be found by wandering.

VOICE ONE

A few doubting-Thomases chanted:

VOICE THREE

….It will never be discovered.

VOICE ONE

Impatiently each shouted down the others.

VOICE TWO

Silence fell upon them
    and then as one
    they looked up the steep cliff face above,
    they squinted into the raven cave before them
    and turned to appraise the narrow trail
        from where they'd come.
Had they missed a path?
Had they failed to see a clever way over the pass?
Had they disregarded a real or god-given sign,
    an indication,
    a prophet's voice?

VOICE THREE

See,

VOICE ONE

….screamed the doubting-Thomas:

VOICE TWO

The sleeping blind man on the bend below,
the one we said was a prophet,
his staff pointed through the snow.

VOICE ONE

But, impatiently,
several men at the front of the broken column,
expressing the ungainly will of the rest,
plunged into the pupil of the cave.
Torches were lit,
shadows played like chimera on the rough hewn walls,
they passed rusted trucks,
dismantled diggers,
axes, shovels and drills of all sizes and rigors.

VOICE TWO

The ex-miners and engineers
took pleasurable revenge,
eyeing the still and frozen objects
whose teeth, ribs, blades and bores had been
    for so many years
their sustenance and tormentors.

VOICE ONE

Here,
after years of forgetting the feel of steel in a callus-
covered hand,
they saw these allies from their long past struggle to
make ends meet,
abandoned,
brought low –
    low like them in their shared history –
yet ragged as they were
the men had survived,

ragged and woolly like the furred rust of the silent tools,
but they were still animate and filled with purpose
to dream of a world
in which they –
    not their tools –
would matter.

VOICE TWO

Their breaths rasped,
their boots splashed,
their tripping pranging knocking sliding and slipping
became an accompaniment to the libretto of their grunts
complaints, expletives –
    and prayers lipped almost soundlessly –
for fear that in the dark womb of the earth
only the dead and the devil would be present.

VOICE THREE

As the cacophony rose like a football crowd
to their team's goal,
all the men at once
became aware of something between
the whisper of splintering mirrors
and the howl of whistling air.

VOICE ONE

Slowly indistinct murmurs
became echoing words,
one over another
spilling on top as shards of phrases, sentences

and paragraphs
sometimes repeated over and over like a mantra or plea.

VOICE TWO

And each,
in a voice of one of their comrades
gave breath to secrets
    hidden in their dampened hearts,
    wrapped in their colons,
    coiling around their genitals,
unbearable thoughts,
unspoken…

VOICE THREE

…. like a scar claiming justice from a guilty knife,
like bruises accusing the bludgeoning hammer:
    my daughters I loved you,
    I had her, the innocent one,
    the boy I coveted,
    she, the closed-thighed bitch whom I wished had died,
    my father the tyrant should expire in pain…

VOICE TWO

…. and revelations of constipation, piles and puke,
and case after case of this and that hatred,
petty jealousy.
nose picking and masturbatory desire –
    men on their own.

VOICE ONE

Embarrassments exposed,
hidden truths exposed,
forgotten chimeras exposed,
and each man heard the other's voices –

    crystal messengers –

and each turned on his neighbour with accusatory glares
until their own voices glanced from the glistening walls
and they too were pinioned by their fellows' crimson stares…

VOICE TWO

…. compelled to rush further into the glacial hole
they began to run,
some, away from the tormenting voices,
others towards the distant light –

    a speck they prayed would offer silence or salvation –

but none escaped and all were revealed to each other
and by and by as they ran and stumbled
they began –

    the flawed humans they were –

to help each other.

VOICE THREE

They ran and sweated in the chilly air,
their breaths formed icicles
that broke from their beards
and cracked into the jaws and shoulders of men behind,
their hearts pounded as much from the exertion and fear
as from the pursuing mercurial mares

revealing what burdened them,
 disguising distress in tissues of metaphor
as a parade displayed in a torch-lit cavalcade,
moving, half lit,
struggling to be recognised in Caravaggio's pools of light.

VOICE ONE

Their passage through the pitchy tunnel
made raven by the fading torches
was soon illuminated by spattering sparks
leaping from foreheads, chests and groins –
 as from a train with brakes aflame –
they could neither stop nor pump their muscles faster
but only proceed with an invariable speed.

VOICE TWO

Helping hands flailed wildly to grasp
older weaker stumbling marchers
from hitting the hard cold ground,
and each in the end was connected to all the others
by an arm, wrist or shoulder
and here and there the younger or stronger
joined with one another
to chair lift, drag or bodily carry on their shoulders
or in their muscled arms
the weak and fallen,
until each one –
 soaked and revealed to all the others –
came out of the tunnel and into the light of a quiet dell.

VOICE ONE

As when people enter a cathedral or museum,
the marchers were struck dumb by innocent silence
and as if a warning of an undefined but finite future,
the marchers
    exhausted,
    embarrassed,
    some close to collapse,
    others with tears of panic held back,
looked from face to face
searching for someone to say:

VOICE THREE

I understand what has happened,

VOICE ONE

or

VOICE THREE

I know where we are.

VOICE ONE

An old shop steward,
set down by two younger men,
walked towards the spring
and looking in,
spoke softly
drawing the others around:

VOICE THREE

This is the sum of our pain and injury:
>hurt another anywhere in the world and you injure me,
>diminish humanity anywhere in the world
>>and you diminish me,
>
>tell an untruth to anyone and you lie to me

and I am not alone but a part of ….

VOICE ONE

The green silent spring sat amongst pines and oaks,
the breeze stayed itself conspiratorially in the canopy
leaving the water's surface a taunting mirror.

VOICE TWO

The men,
sweaty,
filled with fear,
gathered round
>and with the shop steward's words in their ears
>they glanced down and away and again down,

seeing the others first and then themselves
mirrored upside down, then right side up.

VOICE ONE

The breeze stood away like the devil in the tunnel,
the trout stayed hidden –
>releasing a bubble now and then,

the spring soon rippled with intermingling rings –
>response to response –

as the men's eyes released –

drop by drop,
tears held back by a thousand manly footfalls –
    the grease and oil of their futile marching beat.

VOICE TWO

The old shop steward shouted,

VOICE THREE

Drink,
drink don't stare,
don't commemorate,
don't reflect
but refresh yourselves and recall nothing,
feel the liquid on your lips,
refuse to remember what you were,
reject nostalgia for your pasty flesh and cloudy eyes.

Drink,
feel the liquid on your throat and remember nothing,
think of nothing but now
and this wetness.

VOICE ONE

But it was too late.
The men and women saw what they had become
and understood what the villagers and townsfolk had seen –
    that they, in their hunger, filth and rags
    appeared to be what they had once feared themselves –
    the vision of wandering barbarians,
    outsiders,

aliens,
refugees,
the other,
and like a song dancing through the blood of each:

SINGER

We've left our families, homes and land,
travelling for food and jobs and a bed,
we're brown and white yellow and red.

VOICE TWO

To us we're all the same –
we work or we'll be dead.
Our wants are simple:
> jobs and food,
> books and ideas,
> wise leaders and days to idle away,
> to see our children born and nurtured,
> to eat our jam from the cherry orchard,

but…

VOICE THREE

…We've left our families, homes and land,
travelling for food and jobs and a bed
and as one of us stumbles and scars his skin
he looks at the others and lets out a sound:

SINGER

My god my Katcha
I'm failing.

VOICE ONE

They were certain of the taste of home-made bread,
remembered the odour of their lover's skin,
    the glow of sunrise across the park,
    the moisture in pre-storm air,
now they were only certain of things that they could taste and touch,
while the rest –
    the philosopher's hypothesis,
    the governor's laws,
    the factory owner's promises,
    the priest's and the imam's visions
were stories for tomorrow,
which took them one day closer to death and sorrow.

VOICE TWO

And as the summer clouds passed again
to autumn's shrouds
their voices like darkening leaves
drifted from their bodies wheezing...

SINGER

Oh Ashia my beloved Ashia
I'm forgetting, I'm drying, I'm drowning, I'm failing…

XI

VOICE ONE

In that dell,
as the men stood silently around the spring –
    watched for a moment by the hiding trout –
the book readers, autodidacts, and shop stewards
reminded them there was a road,
and they too had a place on it,
and in the heat of blood,
on highways of blood,
in centuries of blood,
in the name of Mohammed, Moses and Christ
    and any chosen anti-Christ,
in the stead of the endlessly varied Protestant, Catholic
    fundamentalist, Jew,
advocates of the sword and faiths believed true,
leaders had a need for labour and warriors
and the invasion of the Algerian
    Bangladeshi
    Maltese and Turk,
all who had ridden and marched their own long road
were part of the history still untold.
But for the authorities...

VOICE TWO

…. cops and truant officers,
bailiffs, judges, lawyers,
professors, principals and head teachers,
advisors, psychologists
social case workers...

VOICE THREE

…. armies with their marines and flyers, grunts and sailors
tax and customs officials,
vat, vehicle, fire or insurance inspectors,
motor licensing bureaucrats,
dad's and territorial army men and boys...

VOICE ONE

…. had another history –
   'official'
they're told,
and in the echoes of their bureau and barracks
they heard reflected...

SINGER

Oh Odysseus my beloved
I'm failing

VOICE ONE

Bosses with their time sheets, productivity curves,
down-sizing, computerising, bottom-lining, profit-making
   better in the long run, suffering in the short,
   immediate gains,

    futures on grains
    for greater and better profit-making,
whose office doors were as low as a brow depressed,
where time punchers entered with a demeaning bow,
their gaze steadfast on official paper wreaths –
    were their dismissal notices hidden beneath?

VOICE THREE

My god I've given the best of my life.

VOICE ONE

With their gaze fixed
    they couldn't see the angels hovering below,
and they too,
the bosses and the angels
    had an official history –
    biblical we're told.

VOICE TWO

And along the rusting iron railway sheds
whistle voices off of ties and shale laid beds...

SINGER

Oh Marte
I'm failing…

XII

VOICE TWO
One day a great sadness overcame them like a
blanket of snow.

VOICE ONE
They and theirs had witnessed the wars, outrages,
the deaths of children from disease,
wasting illness and various healing lore.
They had seen women raped
and men and animals sodomised,
they had seen black robed and red winged intolerance
seep like opium into warriors' blood,
they had heard philosophers and artists
    celebrate firing squads,
    poeticise the gulags,
    glorify forced labour,
    and finally inventing an encyclopaedia of cruelty
    written throughout the century.
They had seen the floundering of empires,
the rise and refutation of ideologies,
the stringing up of tyrants,
the passing of systems and cults
and throughout they had chosen sides:

VOICE TWO

sometimes opportunism –
    dressed as ideology or noble belief –
sometimes retribution...
and they whispered:

VOICE THREE

Let us repossess the landlord's land.

VOICE TWO

But mostly collaboration was easier
and sometimes because they just didn't give a damn.

VOICE THREE

They dug trenches,
turned lathes,
dropped bombs,
prayed and rejected prayer,
drove tanks and terror through the hearts
of other's villages and towns,
left vast numbers of dead in their wake,
buried so many unknown soldiers
and saw so many acts of unrewarded heroism...

VOICE ONE

…. that now
in the great unified one-world single-market peace
they had set themselves in store
for learning, loving and working,
to discover that within the peace
they had become redundant...

VOICE THREE

re..dun..dant.

VOICE ONE

So polite a way of stealing their homes,
security, culture,
loved ones, gender and sex.

VOICE THREE

Our lives –
    our working, loving, learning lives –
were surrounded by –
    encased within –
the features of our god.

VOICE TWO

Here we have the diabolical god
    forcing us to live a life of thwarted expectations.
There we have a circumscribing god
    forcing us to survive in misery,
as he, incapable or asleep,
disregards us,
and in our confused aspirations
    which inhabit a greeny grassed corner of our
    imaginations
we have god's promise
that tomorrow in heaven...

VOICE THREE

…. it'll be alright.

VOICE ONE

But emptiness and hope travelling shoulder to shoulder,
stalling between the hammered granite boulders
became words whipped like eroded grains of sand:

SINGER

Oh Leonora
I'm failing…

XIII

VOICE ONE
On a day when sorrow covered them like snow,
some,
    seeing the choppers flying low,
    and gates closing their paths,
came to remember
they had been in their former lives...

VOICE TWO
the forgers of the steel,
the temperers of blades,
the saddlers who sewed the seats...

VOICE ONE
…. and knowing that man could fly,
that day,
on the edge of a cliff,
    tired of marching,
    of being blasted in the alpine wind,
they came to remember...

VOICE TWO
…. that they too were women and men...

VOICE ONE
…. therefore capable of flight.

VOICE TWO

The stewards insisted
these people pursue a private affair,
so the rest reluctantly turned their backs
as thirty or so launched themselves into air off the cliffs
some chasing Icarus
and others a long sought rest.

VOICE ONE

Waiting their turn to fly,
a few men with darker skin,
dreamt of olive trees cupped in dry white earth,
red wine
and a song in the evening –
    rotund, melodious.

VOICE THREE

Some men –
    tall and whitey blond –
formed their lips to whisper,
expelling breath like the sizz of fine branched pines
heavy with blue needles in a child's spring.

VOICE ONE

Others, round chested and red bearded,
closed their eyes tight against the aqua mountain granite
and remembered large oak leaves
    like the hands of giant men
    browned by the waning season,
leaping through an autumn swirl
landing on their lover's shoulder.

VOICE TWO

One man lamented
he had experienced love,
seen his children born,
his parents die,
he had suffered separation
from his land and work
and the things of life he knew
and now,
alive in his pain,
knowing nothing of dying,
he grasped:
the only certainty in life was its end.

VOICE ONE

Seeing his life become a shadow
he desired unity of his disparate experiences,
he desired wholeness
    like on a canvas with shadows and light
so he too,
    like the other twenty-nine,
pursued Icarus for a future more sublime.

VOICE TWO

Before his flight he whispered to his dark skinned neighbour:

VOICE THREE

For me,
I used to think of rippling water

like my lover's belly beneath my fingers –
    fingers motor-oil silkened
    with sinews stretched by wrenches –
    straight and strong,
sprouting plantations of blond hair,
fingers mingling with her moulded tufts,
but looking back to that pool in the dell,
my reflection –
    an oil drenched pelican,
cast the memory of touching her,
twisting my fingers around her receptive curls –
    a defilement obscene
    mingled as my fingers are in blood and shit,
and I used to believe we were gods –
gods of motor oil and machines;
but now,
    for this last moment,
I believe all that once I thought was true is false,
and yes I know I'm just mortal dross.

VOICE TWO

So he too,
    like the other twenty-nine,
chased his Icarus.

VOICE ONE

Another man,
    an ex-road sweeper,
who had embraced raindrops –

   his allies in cleaning the streets,
had seen his tears shattering mysteries of crystal and glass
   which were forever clear and bright
but now filthy and frozen like his iceberg daydreams
   and night dreams of swimming in clear sweet streams,
but now in his moment of tears and shattering reflections
he recognised those futile years...

SINGER

His white gloves clean,
his uniform spotless,
his sunglasses glinting like his camera's lenses.

VOICE ONE

Now truth –
   like the brook in the meadow's clearing
was shattered forever like the philosopher's learning.

VOICE TWO

With a last moment to live,
to see the rain,
he could reclaim all he had lost.
He would mark for one moment
what was true and what false.

VOICE THREE

That will be my reward
for this march with its blistering pain.

VOICE TWO

A woman who had,
    while programming computers,
dreamt of becoming worthy:
    someone who tossed coins to beggars,
    gave strangers directions,
    took old folks for Sunday rides.

VOICE ONE

Virtues she held onto like a sword
planted by an explorer in virgin earth...

VOICE TWO

    …. and in her last moment –
    as she watched the screen of the sky –
she configured:

VOICE THREE

Most of us just wanted to live a peaceful life,
not in a world of exile –
    a stateless world,
    a world lived in by strangers,
    at best a world of other's ghettos,
most of us wanted to live without despair and death
where exile became a statelessness
    became a ghetto
    became occupied
    became the other begetting violence.

VOICE ONE

And another marcher rubbed his bristled chin:

VOICE THREE

If I surrender now and fly like my comrades after Icarus…

VOICE ONE

…. but do they really fly? he wondered.

VOICE THREE

Then I forsake not only hope I've held so long,
   so strongly in my heart and groin,
but I forsake my loved ones –
   I surrender them to hardship, alone
without for certain knowing
but somehow sensing my soul has gone.

VOICE ONE

Another had seen in his reflection:

SINGER

The relic of his face…

VOICE ONE

…. once viewed with ardour by his wife
   on the pillow,
     between their sheets,
once a moment cherished
within the eye of the wide-hipped laughing woman
   long dead from an ailment incurable...

VOICE TWO

…. or so the expensive doctor said...

VOICE ONE

but every day she was revisited
through his vision blurred,
hiding behind trees and smog and clouds,
now his memory of her,

    a fragment,
    an electrical impulse,
but he told himself:

VOICE THREE

Survival is my proof of love for her,
that she

    once warm folded flesh,
    a laugh coarse and sweet,
    a drinker with the best of them,
    a dancer light on her feet,

that she existed
and in my survival I force her to continue to be.

VOICE TWO

But he too
    like the other twenty-nine
pursued his Icarus.

VOICE ONE

For all,
the granite mountain

crystal white and pale veined blue,
   always hungry for the wanting spectrum
entombed them in their passage as they flew.

VOICE TWO

The stewards insisted
these women and men pursue a private affair,
and so all the rest turned their backs
as some chased Icarus
and others a long desired rest.

VOICE ONE

For the remaining marchers,
   hands in their pockets grasping holes,
   watching the cobbles and holding the road,
windows kiss the shadows
   of the passing thirty million,
while one lean raggedy man
   throws his head back,
   opens his throat
   with his voice ringing from gutter to eaves,
and roars across the city and its gardens' trees,
across the dry eyed factories and the silent railroad yards,
through the lanes and down the river valleys:

SINGER

Oh Junah
I'm a failing, failing, crying, dying…

XIV

VOICE ONE

At another city limit
the police stopped the marchers on a viaduct,
 the inner city line,
 the bastion between the absorbing subs and the
 urban centre,
 the buffer between the cosmos and nature,
 the old ring route,
and held them fast like a ragged centipede facing a
marble wall.

VOICE TWO

Lights ablaze,
rifles ready,
Black Marias waiting near the well-aimed fire hoses,
stun guns, tear gas pellets, riot helmets, perspex shields
all were ready for the marcher's objections…

VOICE ONE

…. when the mayor, followed by the media hounds,
 in this moment of an approaching election,
  stood firm, formal and square shouldered
  in his beautiful draped but severe grey suit,
  satin blue shimmering restrained conservative tie,
and said:

VOICE THREE

Boys and women too,
we know you're wanderers,
ex soldiers,
ex workers, miners,
dockers, engineers
and the lot
and women too,
although propriety shames me to mention what your charms begot,
and that amongst you travel pimps and gamblers,
syphilitics and HIVs,
but good stock as well as the ends of lines,
folk who have laboured and loved sublime,
sown their seed and fostered some distant memory of eternity,
deserving men and prison fodder,
some clean of life and limb,
others foul filthy from travel, morals and associations,
but we would none the less
    welcome you in other circumstances
    than now prevail in our city,
where social discord fed by race and god
fills streets with blood and hearts with pity,
where our Germans hate our French,
our Serbs despise our Croats,
our Greek orthodox and Russians cross each other
    with the intolerance of brothers,
where milk drinkers and wine guzzlers kill for a forgotten slight,

where the French belittle the Belgians
who despise their own Walloons
who resent the city folk from Amsterdam –
    those with beards and paint brushes in hand –
who piss their passing beer from border pubs into German land,
where the Hamburg protestant publishers –
    residents in stone houses –
rail against the Bavarian Catholic peasants
    who despise and look low upon the Viennese thinkers,
and so on to the Turkish neighbourhoods
where they cook with odours obnoxious to the good burghers
    and their muscled sons,
who see papa's property values decline
and jobs unwanted by them taken by the less sublime,
and all and each in their eternal love of Jesus and the good book
find the few remaining Jews to blame –
    socialists inspiring a godless world of hand-outs
    and beggars insane,
capitalists robbing our own heaven-made hard-earned money
    and always sneaking into our women's beds
    with their unbridled urges and flesh denuded pieces
        and clever heads…
…. so you see boys, for the moment boys
    we cannot welcome you
    but as something other –

obnoxious,
enemies to forge us all as one against you –
    our common enemy.

VOICE TWO

Some marcher shouted:

SINGER

We too are human with our hatreds and dislikes
we too know of boundaries and of borders
we too have come upon our limits.

VOICE TWO

Then mayor cried out:

VOICE THREE

But no!
Each day we –
    here in our city –
avoid our limits and look away
leaving them for the sake of sanity
to witness only in our dreams.

VOICE TWO

The marchers rang out:

SINGER

We're the same,
we here as brown and blond
    red and white,
diverse with symbols for our beliefs –

stars and suns,
crescents and crosses of different proportions.

VOICE TWO

And voids,
some cried here and there.

VOICE ONE

Remember our voids,
our emptiness,
nihilists, agnostics and atheists too.

VOICE TWO

The firemen crinkled uneasily in their long rubber coats,
the cops smirked with expectant desire,
the mayor smiled
    a smile of some self-knowing,
    a smile of power,
    a smile which said –
        in form,
    that he was sympathetic
    amused and moved,
but none the less a smile of the lips alone
    outwardly to the press hounds,
    a smile of a man about to become more electable,
    a man holding the borders of morality and decency,
the smile of a man on a hero's voyage –
    a natural born leader,
    handsome, well dressed, the epitome of reason,
fingers neither under the table
in the till

nor down the cleavage of the rich woman's sable,
a smile on his lips beneath his nostrils
which breathed the odour of popularity and re-electability,
a smile spreading like sparks of cordite.

VOICE THREE

In the name of our god,
common humanity,
reason, justice, order and peace
I ask you boys to turn away.

VOICE TWO

A bath,
some wailed.

SINGER

Water bread and ale ...

VOICE ONE

.... all sang out.

VOICE THREE

Charity, that's charity,

VOICE ONE

.... bawled the mayor.

VOICE THREE

But it begins at home,
for everything there is a season
now turn and turn and be gone.

VOICE ONE

The firemen rustled uncomfortably,
the cops smiled with fulfilling desire –
    for order was their function
    particularly under heroic duress.
Some thought of their wives
    often beaten in drunken rage,
as these brave officers
    bragged about their nightly rampage;
as the firemen –
    in truth –
negligent in the art of wounding others,
wondered if they could whitewash the situation.

VOICE TWO

Marchers shouted:

VOICE ONE

We've seen moralists kill
and immoralists take pity,
we've seen coppers lead revolts
and revolutionaries maim for thrills.

VOICE TWO

The marchers sensed the eager stirring of the police
and they called out:

SINGER

We are you,
    sisters and brothers,

   hope against death,
we are not the others.

VOICE TWO

You firemen and cops know your boundaries,
this bridge, your jobs, your limits because we aren't the others;
without us you have no need for borders and boundaries,
no need for hate and identity cards and holding yards.
Without us you face only emptiness alone,
remitted only by video games and guns
sports and speed
and infidelities.

VOICE ONE

The hounded shaggy men and women
confronting
   or at least facing their destiny –
      an enemy unexpected,
      an opportunity only for the
      square-shouldered politician,
began to call out singly and then in pairs,
and at moments as if a chorus declaring:

VOICE TWO

I too have beaten my wife.

VOICE ONE

We also eat lamb with garlic on Fridays.

SINGER (spoken)

And I with rosemary.

VOICE ONE

And another:

VOICE TWO

I shot my brother.

VOICE ONE

And another:

VOICE TWO

I chopped down the rare hardwood trees.

SINGER (spoken)

And we over here turned them into truncheons.

VOICE ONE

For us,
we painted the bridge from end to end and started again.

SINGER (spoken)

And I who so loved,
    disappointed my grandma,
she was made to pay.

VOICE ONE

And we here contrived to let our father die early
    to inherit the shop.

SINGER (spoken)

And I cut the hair of celebrities and sold the sweepings as relics.

VOICE ONE

And I buggered a boy on a boat at sea.

VOICE TWO

And we over here castrated our enemy,
and we like you, wore uniforms
and sang songs to lift our spirits above the grape.

SINGER (spoken)

And I shot a man I called a joker,
removing his eyes from life with a poker.

VOICE TWO

And we over here drank stale beer and broke plate glass
and then we raped the nuns at mass.

VOICE ONE

This chorus of depravity –
    a cacophony of guilt –
set up an echo like a thousand unbroken tramping steps.
Then the bridge began to buckle and leap,
the firemen from fear and without command
    turned their hoses and began the blast,
the policemen drenched
    dropped to the pavement in fear
and the marchers wetted like ducks at play,
    celebrated danced in maddened rounds

    waltzes crazed old jittering bugs, heavy stepped resounds.
The mayor and the press –
    drenched and fearful, fell away
and the cops now at bay
fled to their town with horror in their hearts –
    pity was paid to their women next day.
The firemen left laughing like drains.
They had become heroes they thought,
washing the marchers clean of stains,
drenching the politician and his hounds,
forcing the police to remember their families in need.

VOICE THREE

The firemen knew they had averted death
and were pleased,
driving away in their beautiful trucks,
hoses wound, steel glinting,
drops of water forming
a thousand mirrors on their waxy surface.

VOICE TWO

They drove away leaving the marchers cleansed
to face the defeated city's revenge,
or to return to their towns or hamlets,
    their riverbeds and flinty plains,
    to the hostile glances of long past neighbours -
        cashiers, petrified virgins,
        and their spinster sister's longing;
    to return to face the neighbours
        who would look upon their journey
        as idiocy and defeat.

VOICE THREE

A waste of time,
>   indulgence cruel
>   and heartless now useless too,
with still no money
you'll rob us like the dirty je…

VOICE ONE

Unspoken but agreed,
one by one
the marchers –
>   seeing their clean faces and spotless clothes,
>   silken beards and hair,
dared for a moment to admire each other and themselves.
Speechless murmurless smiles broke out
and one by one while swinging their heads
>   one way towards the city
>   and the other towards the country
>>   they had for so long marched across,
they sat down,
>   straight legged,
>   cross legged,
>   flat on their bottoms or on their haunches,
>   they sprawled or hunkered down,
but one by one,
as if in accord,
they sat.

SINGER

Minutes passed, then hours then days.

VOICE ONE

They could neither think nor speak
　　as if trapped,
but for the rolling hunger of their stomachs
there was silence.

VOICE THREE

No one spoke,
no one wished to speak,
they had exhausted language.

VOICE TWO

No words in German, French, Italian, Spanish,
Basque, Walloon, Flemish, Czech,
Slovak, Serbian, Algerian,
patois this or that
could express anything more
than could their silence.

VOICE THREE

Their pasts and futures joined on the bridge
　　above the fast running water:
life as dreams.

VOICE ONE

Life as dreams –
　　staunch guardians of the truth to some,
　　unreasoned nightmare images to others,
　　wells of forgetfulness to a few.
Created by ideology and advertising,

by love and destruction and religion,
by food and drink and old fashioned habits,
by falling fleeing hunting screwing –
    life-eluding emptiness.

VOICE TWO

Realising these were dreams of unlived life
    to pass the time of day,
    to distract them from the vision of darkened
    corridors.

SINGER

Dreams and emptiness met
in silence but for the river below,
and the distant hum of the humbled city
silence but for their pounding hearts
filled with anguish and with pity.

VOICE ONE

Silence,
    silence filled with memory
    to recall
that for them to survive –
    as least in a thought or two,
meant those who remained alive –
    lovers and children, parents and friends
would remember…

SINGER

…On some bridge,
at some cold dawn
when they slipped into sleep
    sitting above an unnamed river
    in an unnamed country
at that moment
their loved ones were
    or were no longer…

VOICE TWO

So staying alive,
marching across the valleys,
over the mountain's ridges
had continued to protect the existence of their lives and lovers,
and now
one by one
as the days became weeks
the curious townspeople gathered –
    some sold tickets to others for a better vantage,
    restaurants and crèches opened,
where here and there a little porch or platform
offered a view,
and the news gatherers and hounds set their tripods…

VOICE ONE

…. as one by one the women and men at last
whispered…

SINGER

Alzubra I'm failing…

VOICE ONE

…. and turned her eyes away…

SINGER

Bassam my lovely, I'm failing…

VOICE ONE

…. and dropped her head…

SINGER

Ilinka by beloved I am failing…

VOICE ONE

…. and closed his eyes away from the emptiness.

SINGER

hums….

About the author

Robert Golden was educated at Monteith College, Wayne State University in Detroit, Michigan, studying intellectual history for which he was nominated as a Woodrow Wilson Scholar. He continued his education at University of Michigan gaining a degree in Modern European History with a second degree in Design.

He began his career photographing for record covers, magazine illustrations and photojournalistic assignments in New York and London. Robert's work was seen in the London *Sunday Times* and *New York Times* magazines and many other including *Nova* and the *Radio Times*. His photographs have been shown at the V&A, Serpentine, Hayward, Barbican, The Photographer's and other galleries around the UK.

His first feature film 'BEG' was chosen as Best of the Festival at the Edinburgh Film Festival and was selected for Sundance, amongst other festivals in Scotland, Hong Kong, Portugal, Austria and elsewhere. He has written and filmed 35 documentaries, mostly concerned with culture and politics. They have won awards and seen by millions of people around the world.

Robert has also written three plays, a poetry cycle, eight feature film scripts, a series of ten award winning children's books published by Kestrel called 'The

People Working Series', four books about photography and another about unemployment.

Amongst his many documentaries are two concerning children and young people suffering from trauma as a result of war or conflict and the uses of music and the creative arts to support their recovery.

'A Gift of Culture' has been shown at the Davos World Economic Forum and at various international seminars including for the Anna Lindh Foundation at the Organization for Security and Cooperation in Europe. A more recent film, 'Candles Against the Night' has been used to advocate for young people. Robert is currently working on a series of essays called 'Why?'.

For more information please visit:
www.fillingthebox.com

About the publisher

Triarchy Press is an independent publisher of alternative thinking (altThink) about government, finance, organisations, society, complexity, movement, walking, performance, somatics, the future and the creative life.

www.triarchypress.net